Stars

STARS

Poems by

C. G. Hanzlicek

A Breakthrough Book
University of Missouri Press
Columbia & London, 1977

University of Missouri Press, Columbia, Missouri 65201
Library of Congress Catalog Card Number 77–270
Printed and Bound in the United States of America
All rights reserved
Copyright © 1977 by C. G. Hanzlicek

Cataloging in Publication data on last page

Grateful acknowledgment is made to the editors of the following publications, where some of the poems originally appeared:
Choice, "Among Mountain Men"; *Crazy Horse*, "Submarine"; *Hudson Review*, "Stars" and "Oraibi"; *The Iowa Review*, "In a Valley"; *Ironwood*, "Twelve Years Old I Go Rowing at Dawn"; *Poetry Northwest*, "Evening in Los Angeles"; *Poetry Now*, "Canyon de Chelly" and "Eclipse"; *Quarterly Review of Literature*, "Survival"; *The Remington Review*, "Calibrations"; *TransPacific*, "What I Want Is"; *West Coast Poetry Review*, "Academy Cemetery" and "Homeless as Men."

The poems in parts IV and VI first appeared in *Living In It*, a limited, fine press edition, by The Stone Wall Press.

"Mirage" first appeared in *The North American Review*, copyright © 1972 by the University of Northern Iowa.

For Dianne

The Devins Award for Poetry

Stars is the 1977–1978 winner of The Devins Award for Poetry, an annual award originally made possible by the generosity of Dr. and Mrs. Edward A. Devins of Kansas City, Missouri. Dr. Devins was President of the Kansas City Jewish Community Center and a patron of the Center's American Poets Series. Upon the death of Dr. Edward Devins in 1974, his son, Dr. George Devins, acted to continue the Award.

Nomination for the Award is made by the University of Missouri Press from those poetry manuscripts selected by the Press for publication in a given year.

Contents

I

Stars

It's been estimated that atoms
in your body have been through
several stars—that they were
ejected many times as gas from
exploding stars.
                —Jeremiah P. Ostriker

Seattle
Chief of the Suquamish and Duwamish
Said when a white man dies
He no longer loves the earth
He wanders among the stars
Shedding his life
Skin by skin
Until there's nothing but a shiver
Of light

But when a red man leaves the earth
He never forgets rivers
White with a new year
Deer dancing through scrub oaks
The hawk
Shaking the sky with its shriek
And the man often drifts down
To breathe the air of the living
To touch stone
Touch water

Crouched at the firepit
Of an abandoned camp in the hills
With my thumb I polished
The obsidian knife I'd found
Something moved through the pines
Almost like wind

It touched my hair
Then ran downhill to drink at the stream
If it wasn't the spirit of a man
It was at least a spirit of silence
We have lost

I want to move
Quietly on this earth
Touching stones
The trunks of trees
The moons on ponds at night
Touching hair and touching flesh
Almost like wind
And when I die
I won't be ready for stars
They'll have to bury me

Oraibi

*Oraibi is the oldest continuously
inhabited town in America.*

The long cobalt sky
Patches of thin cloud
That would darken and build rain
For a song

Climbing Third Mesa
Sage clumps move closer to each other
The rocks take on weight

North of the highway
From red earth
A sudden island of sand
White as salt
Then once more the color of the people

On the dirt road into Oraibi
I'm met halfway by a sign
Whites may not enter
Because we cannot obey
Hopi laws
Or our own laws

The town raised
Rock by rock out of the earth
Holds the shape
Of mesas outlined in the distance
Holds the color
Of the land at its feet
Almost lost
In what surrounds it

It's a town built on silence too
As I pace
The dust on my side of the sign
I hear nothing
But my own scuffles
Someone in there
Must be singing though
Because clouds
Are moving over the mesa
An eagle swoops through them
Guiding them
Stacking them up like stones
For the Hopi
The Peaceful Ones

Thomas Bunyacya, Medicine Man of Oraibi

He shows me a perfect ear
Of blue corn
From last year's crop
Blue corn he will not eat
During the days of gathering strength
In the kiva

O you've got to fast
He says
You've got to fast to make rain
You've got to be pure

The young ones
Work too quickly
They say let's have a rain dance
Tomorrow
They don't fast for three days
They bring
Windstorms and hail every time

Canyon de Chelly

1.

At the Chinle Shell
The Navajo boy at the pump
Asks if I want my windshield washed
He says I never like to do it
Without asking
Some white men you just touch
Their car
They chew on your ass for an hour

2.

On the east side of town
Hills roll
Their shoulders out of the sand
Men hunker
In the clumps of dusty sage
Like flocks of crows

Unlike crows they have nothing
To say to each other
Staring straight ahead
They roll the brims
Of their sweat-soaked hats

Their hard eyes draw a bead
On the trading post
Its parking lot is lined
With empty pick-up trucks
Navajo Cadillacs
The trader calls them

It's the day checks come in
But they'll ring the hills
Wait there
Not with that rug-stealing
Horse-fucking
Sonofabitch who runs the store

3.

The rock is smooth
And slopes like the top of a skull

From the canyon floor
I must look
Like some parasite of the scalp
Foraging for a vein

In a way I am

Me
The poor seer
Who can't tell eagle from hawk

The poor speaker
With no words to soften an enemy
Or turn a bitter wind

The poor listener
Deaf to the story that drifts
Through the muscles of a fine horse

A man apart
And knowing only that
Driven to sacred land to find
Men apart
Who live for nothing more

And they are here

After all the yellowed weeds
Land green
On both sides of the river

On the far side a single hogan
And a man walking
His five horses to water

On this side
A whole family burning brush
The straight plume
Of their smoke vanishes
Before it can climb the canyon wall

What climbs the wall
Is a solitary crow

Landing on the brow of my rock
He tilts his head once
To take me in
Then turns and walks away

I get your message crow

Downhill to Chinle
A man walks the shoulder uphill
His face so serious
His wife five steps behind
Silent

II

Bend or Break

1.

When I took the powder
Of the moon
Into my insulated hands
And held it up
I found nothing to believe in

Drifting back to earth
Like a spore shot from its cannon
I dream of a jackrabbit
Dead beside a river
Dream of drifting through his ribs
And taking root

2.

A clock in the reed bed ticking
The muskrat diving
Under his V trail for weeds
Leaves baring
Their spines in the shallows
And against the night sky
Whirling clusters
Of fireflies

A whole future
Along the green turn in a river
Where willow limbs
Bend or break above the water

Homeless as Men

Milkweed pods split their skins
My knees tap them
They send out plumes of down
Some find their way to the soil
Others on my pantlegs
Are homeless as men

Toward evening the sun draws blood
From the belly of the earth
A deer drinks at a red pond
And then folds its legs
In a bowl of grass

In firelight
The bat who hung all day like a glove
From a limb his color
Trembles
And dips a wing into night

This hour used to send men to their beds
I light a lantern
Lie awake for hours to its hiss
Imagining the rising sun
I'll sleep through

In a Valley

The sun clutches the grey rim
Of the mountains
Like a man climbing out of a well

The down on my wife's face
Turns to a skin of light

I nudge her awake
As the owl above us turns his head
Preparing for silence

We hold a silence too
But a pine knot pops in the fire
And he glides off to a further tree

We'll be alone again today
Teaching animals how to keep a distance

We bow to drink at the creek
Rise with the green blood of grass
On our knees

Among Mountain Men

Coming out of a curve a coyote
Is nailed to a fence
His four shoulders broken
Spine flattened against the post

Trailing blood and feathers
He dragged chickens to his gulley
Until he was emptied into this

In these yellowing hills his eyes
Shrink to raisins
The tongue dries to a strip of jerky
And his stomach
Draws to the walls of its cavity

Strapped in my seat
I lick dust from my lips and drive on
To weeds the color of clay
Drive on to the next hour among men
Whose love is a law
To be broken like bones

At a Lake In Minnesota

Walking the shore toward me
Is the farmer from across the road
A man with seven teeth
And forty acres gone to weeds
The bib of his overalls supports
A belly bloated
By pilsner and boiled potatoes

Each fifty paces or so
He baits and sets a steel trap
Tells me he's after muskrats
Says these days their pelts ain't worth
A nickel in a whorehouse
But the varmints ruin
The shoreline with their nests

This is a man who *owns* things
His body his mind
A lake and every foot of its shore
And if a woodpecker
Breaks through his sleep at dawn
A little jolt of birdshot
Will wipe it away
Clean as a fog of breath
Leaving his shaving mirror

After he's rounded the point
I get the broom from the cabin
Beginning where he began
I touch the broomstick
To the baited tongue in each trap
A loud clack moves over the water
A satisfying sound
A life saved
A whole shoreline gone to hell

Mirage

The scrape of my feet is an alarm
The lake tips its mirror
Pours its silver into a canyon

A light wind shimmers the sky
Like a sheet of foil

A man who can drink light
Drink silver
Can stomach anything
I confess now my love of water

The cactus army
Throws up its arms in surrender
Waves a flag of vultures

Without knocking a pack rat
Walks through the door
Of a snake

Without knocking
I walk all day through myself
Yesterday I was here
About tomorrow I've said too much

Nautilus

The sea has written a story on the shell
In lines of brown ink

The characters turn inward
And then vanish in a darkened chamber

Hold it to your ear
And you hear only one long breath

To know how the tale ends
You'd have to smash the shell on a rock

It must be read like the story of a man
With no desire for an ending

Silence

There was a moment last winter
When I was sure it was silent here
Now the breath of a new winter
Grazes my eyelids
And a small animal breaks deeper
Into hard brush
The drying leaves
Reach for each other and cough

Sometimes I want to hold
Silence like a small animal
Hold it so tightly its eyes widen
And I begin to fear myself

But it's escaped me
Its heart throbbing like a cut thumb
To the higher ridges
Where the wind can't find its way
Into pine boughs

I'm left with a narrow stream
That hisses across pitted granite
Like a fire of green wood
Left with a fire
That won't fall into silence
Until there's nothing left to burn

III

Twelve Years Old I Go Rowing at Dawn

Pulling through lily pads
A cry from the wall of reeds
Cry like the screech
Of the oarlocks
The turtles duck their heads

Loon is up early too
He rows his boat on a lake
Of fog
Yanks his old oars like wings
Yodeling yodeling
Too crazy to be afraid

Getting so thick I can't see a thing
But the wet prow
The anchor
Bleeding weeds
On the front seat

How deep is it here
A big hole
A giant pike down there
Kicks up sand with his tail
Spits a necklace
Of minnow bones

I can't see but that black shape
Is the back maybe
Of a moose
Rising for the third time
Pull right pull right

Call me one more time one more time
Old man loon
I'll drop my oars
Take a walk
Follow you

Calibrations

His shoes slick and soft with oil
Caked by curled steel shavings
Were docked like boats for a week
On newspapers by the door
When a disc
Lost its place in his spine

Eyes bright with animal pain
He crawled
On hands and knees through the house
Cried when he had to rise
Into the shape of a man
To take a piss

With a little fear still in his eyes
He went back to the factory
To feed steel stock
Into his milling machine
To live by close tolerances
Exact measurements

Nights in his basement workshop
When he pulled a beaded chain
The bare bulb swung
Our shadows from wall to wall
I sat on a box
And watched him get lost
In the softness of wood

Often I'd ask to see his calipers
Their leather case
Was slick with his own oil
The numerals and lines
Had all worn smooth
Under the ball of his thumb
But for him the calibrations were clear
In his memory
In the sureness of his touch

The Drive-In Movie

for Terry Allen

Beyond the last row of speakers
Out in the marshy field
Where bullfrogs

Barked against the soundtrack
A light
Topped a thin steel tower

A pale greenish light
Advertised as a dependable moon
For the lovers among us

My friend knew a girl in another car
In the back seat of his Model A
A car with window shades

I sat alone with my hands
And felt lime-flavored vodka
Turn and turn within me

I threw the speaker out the window
And pulled the shades
Against both our small-town moons

The one burning above a marsh
The other burning
Beyond all my understanding

The lower moon was at full phase
I didn't long for love
I was too young to give back to it

I cried my drunken cry
Just to be touched and to feel
A release the small animal knows

Chased by dogs through underbrush
Then stumbling into its burrow at last
To draw free breath

Submarine

. . . submarines, the snouted voyagers
of the sea's unconscious . . .
—Malcolm Lowry

What is outside
Is enough pressure for steel to burst
And then close upon itself
Like a lung at sixty thousand feet

It grows stronger as you drift down
Into the murk
Until only the hardest-shelled creature
Can hold it away

And at the intricate bottom
Where sand
Is pulled into ridges
Like the landscape of a brain
Your friends might suddenly betray you
For a little love
They thought they had coming

What is inside
Is dark
Dark as a squid's blossom of ink
That will not be written into anything
You can read

When I was seventeen
My grandfather dived through a hole
Into sleep
I began to think I'd found a calling
Among the strange men
Who rolled the sod back over him

I must have thought
If I touched waxy flesh every day
Pushed arms hard as lumber
Into new shirts with the backs ripped open
Wired jaws shut
Against any last silence
They might open to

I must have thought
Then I'll know it
I'll know it so well I can betray it

It takes a long time
To rise even to the surface of things
To the gulls wheeling
In the trail of vegetable peels
The soft shell of the sky before dark
And the long laughter of waves
And then the horn sounds
Over and over
And someone below shouts
Dive Dive Dive

Evening in Los Angeles

I slide into deeper shadow
As the sun falls off
Its shelf into the sea

Each time I take in air
My lungs rise
Like moons in my chest

In the darkness an old
Despair comes on
Despair that turns to desire

Desire to see the city
Plunge its hands to cool
In a barrel of sweet rain

To see the sun refuse to set
And roads retract
Like the tongues of snakes

To see wood turn to steel
And steel to wood
So wood might win in the end

To see the violently planned
Hills bend at last
To touch the dry earth

Because these desires
Are endings
For a sky that is endless

A sky whose vague stars
Have twins
Failing on the sea's surface

I find myself as on any night
Between the two heavens
Singing a song

About life that divides them
Without an end
Without even a good beginning

IV

Man Waiting

The path is growing
Dark. It is a long
Time between people.

I need a long time
Between people. For
Hours I've been throwing

Pebbles at pigeons
That move like milk. Feed
Them, stone them, bless them,

What does it matter?
What matters is that
All of us are here.

That I am here. Soon
The lamps will glow and
Dusty moths begin

Their nervous orbits.
I'll wait here, out of
Sight, far from benches

And bums whose odor
Burns worse than bread-strained
Sterno. I'll wait here

For the clean light and
For a woman who
Moves like milk. I'll smile

As she sees me turn
To her and open
My raincoat like wings,

Like wings. To be is
To expose oneself—
Head, pecker, and knees.

The Old Man Made It

The old man made it
Past the guards again.
He runs down the street,

Tailed by yapping dogs,
His gown billowing
To bare his skinny

Ass, banging the bottom
Of a cast-iron
Skillet with a spoon.

I remember when
He was sane. He rocked
On the porch all day,

Shooing the sparrows
That shit with care on
His waxed Oldsmobile.

When they came back he'd
Toss them bread, and nod,
And sing himself to sleep.

Then last June he sang
To his pigeon-
Breasted neighbor girl,

And the town put him
Away. Somehow it's
Always me who has

To stop him, chase the
Dogs away, and say,
It's all right, Howard,

Everything's all right.
Arm in arm we jog
Our way to the home.

The cook gets back her
Skillet and her spoon,
I get my thankyou

From the guards, the old
Man gets his red pill.
How strange it's always

Me who stops him, when
I have in my closet
My own sort of bell,

And in my mind, these
Days, a similar
Sense of alarm.

Survival

Once, over beers in Colorado,
I heard about a man
Who slit open
A deer
And climbed inside it
To keep from freezing.

When they found him
They gave him whiskey,
And while they cut
Off his feet
He bit down hard on a knifeblade.

A fool in Colorado,
Who keeps cases filled with souvenirs,
Can show you the teethmarks
On your face
In the steel.

And how will we make it,
The fool and I,
With feet that squirm in our shoes
And mouths full of teeth
Like mush?

How will we survive,
Now that the sack
Of nails
Has left the hand, and the whole
World's floor
Is inside us?

What I Want Is

What I want is
Enough money

To have what I want
What I want is

My own hill
And beneath that hill

A pond
In the pond a lazy

Bass or two
And duck feathers

Resting on the mud
Of the shore

Between the hill
And mud a patch

Of grass where I
Can lie and count

My seven trees
My seven clouds

And count the coyotes
Coming down the hill

To drink
Coyote 1 Coyote 2

How To Care

His wife's belly is
Swelling.
She is seven months pregnant.
His daughter's
Belly is swelling,
And she is three years old.

His hut has no table,
No closet, and no shelf
For an ivory
God to stand on.

He owns a bone-handled knife,
But the talk
Of the insects makes no sense:
He's out for flour
Not for blood.

The priest who moves
Like a tree dressed in black
Brings him a package
From Santa Barbara.
He finds a transistor radio,
A diamond, and a note:

Do you understand what it means
To have a better life?
We give you these keys.

He plays the radio.
What a difference music
Makes, he says.

He looks down into the long
Corridors
Of the diamond.

Inside he sees the clean
Streets and white
Houses of Santa Barbara,
And inside Santa Barbara
He sees two stomachs

Bulging like late summer melons.
Yes, he says, yes.
O god, he says.
He says, O god, how strong

My back must have been
To carry my family
Into the hardness of that city.

V

Salt

The catfish can taste with its skin
A blunt snout scoops
Through the bottom murk of the Mad River
Carried along in a walk to the sea

One day it goes too far
And the creamy belly skin says
Salt salt salt
And the dark tail swirls muscle
Against the boiling currents

One day a woman walks too far on the beach
She opens her blouse to the sea
And the nipples say
Salt salt salt
As they wrinkle and darken

The sudden spray off a black rock
Walks into her body
Like a knife
Behind her the Mad River hisses
In its last run across sand
The wind lifts the hair from her neck
And then moves inland in search of trees

Whole worlds die off in such moments
But it would be another thing
To see trees
Stop for her green eyes
To see the last drifting fall
Of her blond hair
That will go on growing for nothing
Ashes to dust
Dust to skin that tastes of salt

Academy Cemetery

for Philip Levine

The stones are old
Mostly from the nineties when a plague
Snuffed out the candle
In the moon
And stole across the yards of farms
To kiss the children
In their beds

A pink plastic rose with a spider
For a stamen
Opens forever beneath the words
Baby has gone home

The hill is bare of grass
The soil rises inside small whirlwinds
And roots are left above ground
As if the trees want to walk away
I want to walk away
I want to go home
By home I mean a wooden house
I lock each night

Belief

I want to speak of a father
Bible-struck
Who as an act of faith
Flushed
His son's insulin down the toilet

At a prayer meeting
A woman held the boy's head
While sugar
Gathered to throw him into shock

The kid started crying
Shook the fat of her arms
When her eyes showed only whites
And she spoke in tongues
Like a turkey damned to the block

In two days the ax fell all right
But on the boy
And his head rolled off the pillow
Into his father's arms

His body was laid out
Minus flowers
Minus grief
On the kitchen table
For him to rise on the third day

But the boy
Would not let go
The sullen stone of his sleep

Bed of Nails

1.

Child could say twenty words
But mostly said no no
Crawled the carpet like a swollen snake
Ticking its tongue
Against chips of teeth

Wife could say a thousand words
Make him want to hide his face
Behind stubbed fingers
Cup his knotted groin in his palm
Drive nails
With his fist

Night shifts he stacked cartons
On wooden pallets
When he punched out the last time
He left his card in the clock

Went out to bury a quart of whiskey
In the folds of his liver
Buried a car in a storefront

Walked off snapping
His hands at the wrists
As if he wanted to knock
Rings from his fingers

2.

I watch the moon drive silver
Nails into the grass

He runs from the house laughing
The air around his head
Claps its hands

When he falls
There is a spot like a birthmark
On his temple

I shout his name
And his terrier barks twice

The air sharpens
As the sirens zero in

His wife sticks a knuckle in her mouth
And tries to weep
The terrier whines at her knees

And I whine to my wife
About a man's life and a dog's
And how the two can come together
On a bed of nails

He's wrapped in a sheet
Strapped down
Loaded like a shell into a cannon
Shot into the country of his choice

3.

Light sweeps ashes from the blanket
A breast brushes
The snowfield of the sheet

I want to stay in bed
But with eyes open
To tiny blue rivers under the skin
That flow through a woman's life

In those old winters
Alone in bed
When morning snow was flecked by soot
When I called to myself in shadows
And wanted to die
I must have known this could happen

A woman
A shadow-gatherer
Who if she means to lie will not talk

The skin across her brow
Loosens as she speaks
The first words of this morning

Four Poems for Dianne

1. *Lake Frances, Minnesota*

With her fins the sunfish carved
A bowl in the sand
Laid her bright yellow eggs
Then left as the male
Hovered over them
When his cloud of sperm settled
He circled the eggs on guard

On our bellies on the dock
We watched his week-long vigil
Magnified by clear water
His own kind made raids against him
He'd charge one
Chase it into weeds
Return to two in the nest
Pecking eggs and spitting sand

Constant and alone
He saddened us
We dropped earthworms and fat grubs
Into his bowl
But he wouldn't pause to eat

Then one night a storm
Whipped the lake into whitecaps
At dawn the bitten shore
Was lined with uprooted weeds
He was gone
The eggs had been torn away
By something he couldn't charge

We took the canoe out in silence
Our paddles sliced
The muddied water to the same rhythm
The boat cut a straight line
To maple woods on the point
Where a week before we'd watched
A pair of belted kingfishers
They'd made their dives
From the very top of a tree
To break water like ax heads
Hunting together

2. *The End of Dormancy*

It was the middle of March
Roots that kept
To themselves all winter
Began to crawl
Out the drainage holes
They printed strange tracks
On the white saucers beneath them

At the kitchen table
You jumped them to larger pots
I watched your breasts
Sway inside your T-shirt
As you knocked the plants loose
From their old walls

You trimmed the root clumps
With a butcherknife
Settled them into the pots
Tamped handfuls of soil

For a week nothing
Then buds
Broke through along the stems
The house filled with new leaves
Their shadows
Softened the white walls

I crawled out of myself
Broke through
To the power of your body
Your hands that shape a season

3. *Our Skins Won't Hold Us*

He comes to us
Cupping darkness in his hands
We offer him coffee
When he tips the mug to his mouth
A moon on the dark water
Floats toward his lips
He will not drink
He pulls on a coat of loose threads
Rounds a corner into night

Alone
Our lungs release rough air
Our shoulders meet
Your breasts burn
Like wings
On a hawk's first flight
When we fly into each other at last
Our skins won't hold us
What we think we are cries out
Glides from our circle
To lose itself in darkness

It could be we're learning death
The body lost in life
Meets only itself in flight
And cannot bear it
The wings open
The body takes a last deep breath
Then soars
Into its own darkness

4. *Last Wish*

When my hands shrink
From all that has held them

When my eyes take no light
To bring you into me

When my heart closes
And won't let go its blood

When everything in me
Finds its level like water

Don't take a last look at me
I was another man

VI

A Toast for the New Year

Among the dry rattling stands
Of cornstalks
Pheasants peck out
Each other's eyes.
This is their last hope
For justice,
But even blindness won't stop
The hunters
Sweeping the field,
Their blasts tumbling the birds.
The game is
Nailed by its wings to the fences,
The men pose
For photographs.
I drink to them and to blindness
Of the fields in daylight.

And I drink to the girl
In the sixth-floor room who poses
For a pornographer.
Spread them a little wider, he says.
She grins into the tense eye
Of the camera,
Spreads until the muscles quiver.
Her name is Bobbie Kane.
I drink to Bobbie,
The girl who lives on walls
Nobody's going to touch.

I drink to the photo of me
Naked,
Painted a bright blue,
Beating a drum
To which no one in the background
Dances.

I drink to the river of my childhood,
River half in, half out
Of love,
River where carp
Float lazily toward the dam
Belly up.
I touched my first girl there
Among weeds,
The round fish,
And the moon
Breaking and forming again
And again on the water.

Under a ceiling of roots
Young men toss
In their sleep for fear.
Train tickets turn
To powder in their fists.
Their women wait under trees,
Write the same words
In their diaries each night.
I drink to the war
The men thought they were fighting,
The one they knew would be written about,
And to the care
Of their women's words.

I drink to insects
Kissing the plants good-bye
In the first
Frost of the year.

I drink to the landlady
Whose husband died of cancer.
She keeps one room for herself.
There she draws delicate
Studies of toads
That lick flies from the air
For food.

I drink to the man
In the bus station who pays
A dime to weep
In a toilet stall.
The others
Stand at the sinks for hours
To comb
Their long brown hair.

I drink to the street called Gabriel
Where a taxi is parked at the curb.
Someone checks off our names
As the meter runs.
On the corner a man
Identifies himself to a uniform,
Pulling card
After card from his wallet.

I drink to the sirens in the night
Speeding toward open wounds,
And to dogs
Whose howls rise in pitch
Until they become
Sirens.

A woman sits among dirty plates,
Old calendars,
A rootbound philodendron.
She counts beads in the light
From a window.
This prayer is for my husband
Sweating glass
Beads in the forge shop,
Shaking in the fall
Of the drop hammer.
And this prayer is for my daughter
Who married the right foot

On a punch press pedal
And a Christmas bonus.
I drink to that woman.
I can't pray.

I drink to the painter
Brewing coffee beside blank canvas,
Waiting to make his move,
Who knows if he paints red
It is a lie,
Yellow too is a lie.

I drink to my own lies,
To my one last star
That is falling,
To all the living, all the dead,
A long drink,
A drink to last a lifetime,
This drink of pain
In the world
That insists on it.

VII

Eclipse

1.

When I was a child on a small town's edge
I was carried on a light wind
Through the marshes
I learned frog and milkweed
Snake and willow
Uncovered a grassy nest
Of fingertips
Tended by a trembling mouse

One autumn night
I felt a strong wind
That lifted and sounded
The tin gong of the streetlight
Shaking out pieces of light
That jumped through maple leaves
The leaves clattered
Down the street and southward
Like a fast freight
Bearing a cargo of air

Above it all
At an altitude of calm
A wide and silent V of geese
Crossed the moon

2.

Black boxelders stripped of leaves
Couldn't hold back the wind
It rattled the windows
Seemed to shove
The whole weight of the house
Until the joists moaned
The nights I was alone in the house
I took a knife to bed
And breathed more smoothly
When a full moon turned snow
To the skin of a sleeping face

When the oak stairs creaked
I knew what I feared
Was not taking off its shoes for silence
Or watching its hands whiten
On the banister
To steady its next step
It was inside me
Pacing the cage of my ribs
Saying close your eyes
You're so alone
You might as well close your eyes

3.

In the nursery field after the dance
My dad's Chevy
Made the new snow groan
We parked between careful rows
Of pine and spruce
Such clear air
The moon broke through so bright
We saw an owl
Glide on the wind between trees
To peel a mouse from the snow

We kissed
Kissed until the windows fogged
Kissed until KDHL went off the air
Kissed until our lips
Were swollen and blue with bruises
Kissed until my heart
Flopped like a dying duck
My groin was such a strange
And burning gnarl
I never wanted to kiss again

I walked her to her door
We kissed
Back at the curb
I grabbed
The Chevy's cold rear bumper
Tried to lift
The car right off the road
Afterward I felt better
But I still hated a body
A girl couldn't take to her body

4.

My grandfather grew up in Bohemia
Summers he watched the dawn
Rise between wind-rounded hills
To strike a stubborn farm
Winters he broke
His back in a brickyard

One day the farm laid
Down to die
The brickyard ran out of straw
And he found himself in Minnesota

A machinist
Who aged into a janitor
Raising a family he loved
To give advice

To my father
Never let a man buy you a drink
If you were starving
The same man
Wouldn't buy you bread

And to me
Take all the politicians in the world
Put them in a big paper bag
Shake them up
And you'll get
A shit-ass on top every time

In the end he was tortured
For half a winter in the hospital
A man of kindness
Who in death turned to anger

All the saints moved through his fever
But they brought
No comfort down
From the hills of his pain
He ripped
The catheter out of his penis
Jumped out of bed
To curse their names

He made it home for a few days
Sat on the edge
Of his bed watching nuthatches
Slam his sunflower seeds
Into folds of bark against a hard time

Despite his wishes
He was buried with Christian rites
Buried in the old Bohemian cemetery
Where on weekends
He'd once dug graves

It only took
Ten turns of a winch
To put him away for good
A wind knocked snow from pine boughs
It drifted down inside my collar
To teach my spine
How cold he was

5.

A dark side grew in me
So dark
It moved through me
Like a total eclipse of the sun
Light going from yellow
To burnt orange to brown
Everything fading in the cone of shadow
Always afraid
I was always afraid
And nothing seemed to touch my fear

6.

Chuck
I'll only tell you this a hundred times
So listen carefully

It's time you walked like a man
Walk through pain Chuck
It can't touch you
Walk through it like so much milkweed

Walk through love
It can't touch you
Walk through it like so much rain

Walk through death
It's just a long sleep of snow
That melts your flesh

And any dreams you've got
Can be bought downtown
For a buck

With a little work
You can own your future
Nothing can touch you
You can learn to wake from death
You can learn to live alone
Nothing can touch you
You can have a future clear and clean
Clean as a full autumn moon
A flock of geese
Wouldn't dare to cross

7.

Under an orange evening sun
In the perfect air of San Francisco
In a little park
Across from a sand-colored church
I saw a man on a bench
Well-dressed
Alert
With an attaché case on his knees
He had an orange in his hand
And he smashed it
Again and again hard on the corner
Of the black case
Until he and the leather
Were covered with its juices

I won't say it didn't touch me
But I was more moved
The day my wife and I stood in the window
Watching the sun settle
Behind a peach tree
A strange wind
Brought a pair of grosbeaks
One right after the other
To our window
Dianne screamed
They hit so hard
Against our faces in the glass

Their trembling in the flowerbed
And the final twitch
That wrapped their bodies in their wings
Wrapped me in the life
Of the woman who stood beside me

There is nothing
Nothing I want to believe in
There's the woman who enters my fear
Like sunlight breaking through trees

There are deaths I could choose
So tangible
A bank would help me finance them
And there is the death
That will choose me
Invisible
Shivering like a pane of glass
In a high wind

I'll wait to be chosen
I'll wait with my one belief

Library of Congress Cataloging in Publication Data

Hanzlicek, C   G   1942–
   Stars.

   (A Breakthrough book)
   I. Title.
PS3558.A544S7   811'.5'4   77–270
ISBN 0–8262–0226–8